Your Best Marriage

Other titles by Dale Sadler

No More Yelling:
Tactics for effectively
communicating with your teen

28 Days to a Better Marriage:
Advice on how you can have the
relationship with your spouse that you've
always wanted.

Generations to Come:
Becoming all things to your child
(Available at www.21stcc.com)

Your Best Marriage

by

Dale Sadler
Licensed Professional Counselor
Mental Health Service Provider

Table of Contents

PART 1   1

CHAPTER 1 – MARRIAGE PHASES OVERVIEW   3

CHAPTER 2 – DIVORCE   7

CHAPTER 3 – CONFLICTUAL MARRIAGE   15

CHAPTER 4 – DETACHED MARRIAGE   23

CHAPTER 5 – WORKING MARRIAGE   31

CHAPTER 6 – THRIVING MARRIAGE   37

PART 2   43

PART 2 – INTRODUCTION   45

CHAPTER 7 – COMMUNICATION   49

CHAPTER 8 – SELFISHNESS   57

CHAPTER 9 – PARENTING   63

CHAPTER 10 – HOW YOU HANDLE CONFLICT   69

CHAPTER 11 – WHERE IS GOD IN YOUR MARRIAGE?   77

CHAPTER 12 – AFFAIRS AND INFIDELITY   89

CHAPTER 13 – LOVE IS AN ACTION   101

<u>Dedication</u>

To my wife, Malita,

who always makes marriage exhilarating.

Acknowledgements

I would like to thank several people who have had a small or large part in the forming of this work. First, the elders and ministers of the Castle Rock Church of Christ who saw a need to minister better to the families under their charge.

Second, to those who read the manuscript and offered suggestions: my wife, Malita, Matthew Morine, Mark Walker, Danny Camp, and Debbie Bumbalough.

Next, I want to thank my children for being patient with me as I typed away on weekends, during the summer and on snow days at home to get this project completed. May God bless each of you with a kind and supportive spouse some day.

About the Author

Dale Sadler is a Licensed Professional Counselor/Mental Health Service Provider. He has a family counseling practice in White House, TN, where he specializes in marriage, parenting and men's issues. He is also a School Counselor at Portland East Middle School in Portland, TN, and he serves as the youth minister for the Birdwell's Chapel Church of Christ in Cottontown, TN.

As on online curriculum consultant with Renewed Vision Counseling Services, Dale trains other counselors on topics such as ADHD and bullying. Dale is a trained Prepare/Enrich provider, which is an assessment for couples both married and looking to marry.

Dale has worked with children, teens, sex offenders, addicts and couples. He has traveled the country speaking on the topic of marriage and has even been a regular speaker at the Tennessee School Counselors and Administrators Institute where he was recognized for his work with at-risk students. Earning his bachelors in 1999 from Freed-Hardeman University, he went on to Western Kentucky University and earned his master's degree in Marriage and Family Therapy in 2004.

Dale is the author of three other books: *28 Days to a Better Marriage*, *Generations to Come: Becoming all things to your child* (through 21st Century Publishing), and *No More Yelling: Tactics for effectively communicating with your teen*. Dale's writings have been featured in the *The Gospel Advocate*, *Think Magazine* by Focus Press and he has written for the National Center for Fathering at Fathers.com.

Dale enjoys fly-fishing, gardening, hiking and spending time with his wife and two kids.

www.DaleSadler.net

Forward

Dale and I go way back. He was a youth minister, and I was impersonating a youth minister. As I got to know him, I learned that Dale has a knack for amazing ideas. Some of his ideas seem crazy at first, but they always work. One example was the time he rented a community recreation center for a lock-in with elementary school kids. All of the parents believed the idea was nuts but it worked. We had over 150 kids come for an amazing night of fun, devotionals, and way too much coke and pizza. The best part was over 100 kids from the community participated! Elementary kids are not shy inviting friends to a once in a lifetime all-night extravaganza. It was good evangelism.

You do not meet too many individuals that are as highly gifted as Dale. A lot of people have a few interests, a few areas within a wheelhouse of certain skill sets, but Dale is great at everything. He is an accomplished artist, cans his own marinara sauce and he even fly-fishes for wild trout in the Smoky Mountain back-country. So, it is not a stretch for him to write a book. Really, when he sets his mind to a task, he always delivers something amazing. For fifteen years, I have watched him bless churches as a minister, save marriages as a family counselor, mentor students as a school counselor, be an amazing husband and father, and be my friend.

This book is the fruit of years of intentional study through academic institutions. It is through countless hours of counseling couples in chaos and confusion, and most importantly, it is through modeling and practicing these principles in his own home. What you must love about Dale is that everything he writes, he does. No one wants financial advice from a poor man, and no one wants marriage advice from a terrible husband. The advice and wisdom he gives is from a man that is doing more than talking, he is living out these principles. And like his crazy ideas, they work.

The book has been divided into two sections. In part 1, Dale provides a helpful mirror so that couples and church leaders can discern the state of any marriage. He deals with the Thriving, Working, Detached, and Conflictual marriage phases. Each chapter sheds light on the attributes and behaviors of individuals within their marriage. At the end of each of these chapters, there are helpful resources to continue to guide the couple along the journey of having a crazy, great marriage.

The second part of the book shines the spotlight on successful tactics for thriving marriages. After providing the framework of assessment, Dale steps into the practical behaviors of loving couples. These chapters touch on the common areas of marital conflict. No one can read these chapter titles like communication, selfishness, conflict, and affairs without realizing that this material will help every couple become better lovers and partners.

This book is full of ideas, perhaps crazy ideas, but trust me, like every idea Dale has had, it will work for your marriage. It has worked for Dale and the droves of couples he has assisted. So, it will work for you! Besides his wife is not just crazy in love with him because of his amazing hair, it is because he is an amazing man.

Matthew Morine, author of *A Mountain Moving Faith, Teaching Young People to Reach the Ultimate Summit*. He is the pulpit minister for the Castle Rock church of Christ in Castle Rock, CO.

www.MatthewMorine.com

Introduction

After doing a marriage seminar in Castle Rock, CO, I was approached by the elders and ministers there to devise a plan to assist them in their marriage ministry. They needed a system where a lay counselor such as a minister could easily assess a couple, and then recommend useful steps to help the marriage improve. This book is the product of not only that discussion, but a culmination of my experiences with many couples over the years. These couples have moved from one marital state to another.

I have worked with many couples who have moved from near-divorce to a once again thriving marriage. All it takes is dedication, effort and a faith in yourself and in your Savior. It is the wisdom of Scripture that can change a heart and the lives of two broken people.

When I was a Bible student at Freed-Hardeman University, I made the decision to get my master's degree in Marriage and Family Therapy. This decision has enabled me to work in two different fields (counseling and ministry), but it has also enabled me to see a great disconnect between churches and the people who desperately need their help. Elders and ministers with vision will see this, as well. They will see as one by one, families in their congregations suffer in their relationships. They will see these same "strong" families crumble because of infidelity. "I would have never thought he/she would do that." They will see that you must do more than reference Ephesians 5 if you are going to actually save marriages. You must supply families with resources that can move them to a brighter future. I hope this book can be a part of that.

In the last 50 years our society has become increasingly isolated. Some blame technology but this loneliness began way before the iPhone. America has slowly moved away from the village mindset to an independent one. Churches are still tight-knit groups, even cliques; think of your members. How many actually come who are in desperate need of salve for their spiritual wounds? If a family is a mess, they are not likely to let it show; you are not likely to ask. If things aren't going well, a family will more than likely drop out of attendance or go elsewhere. While churches aren't supposed to be counseling agencies, they do have the love of Christ and the wisdom of Scripture to help them heal couples. Will they use it?

In each chapter of Part 1 you'll find a description of the phase, behaviors that brought you there and how to move out. I have included books, websites and

other resources. Consider the books I have here, but a quick Google or Amazon search will bring up books that may suit you better. The point is that you can gain skills through reading. Make this a part of your marriage improvement plan.

As I thought about what Castle Rock needed, I began to consider the various couples I see in my practice. These couples are very similar in their journey as husband and wife, and as such

I began to see many patterns emerge. I hope I can identify your marital state in this book, and I pray it sets you on a path to a better marriage; *Your Best Marriage*.

PART 1

--

The Marriage Phase System: Where are you?

Chapter 1 – Marriage Phases Overview

"A successful marriage requires falling in love many times, always with the same person." –Mignon McLaughlin

--

A marriage is a living system that has a degree of health depending on the interactions between the spouses. Like anything living, a marriage changes over time. The spouses change as they mature and this has an impact on their relationship. The key is how do you adapt to these changes? Changes like children, careers and even physical changes of each spouse can move you in or out of the phases. Briefly, these are how the different phases interact with one another. A more thorough explanation of each is given in subsequent chapters.

Typically, a marriage starts in the thriving phase. Some may call this the honeymoon phase, but that suggests you can leave this phase just like you left your cabin in Gatlinburg a few days after your wedding. Honeymoons are temporary, but a thriving marriage can last a lifetime.

Depending on where you are in even a healthy marriage, you can move in and out of each phase. For instance, you might characterize your marriage as working during the years of child rearing. Hopefully, you are in and out of thriving, but for the most part, you would say your marriage is working. You enjoy one another company, but your efforts are not regularly put into the relationship.

Thriving

Working

Detached

Conflictual

Divorce

The detached phase is where marriages can begin to deteriorate. Where you once were regularly engaged with one another, you have grown apart and are being a separate spouse in a legally joined relationship. You begin to develop interests that do not involve the other, and soon your energies are put into things that involve no interaction with your loved one.

Second, while all marriages have conflict to some degree, no healthy marriage is characterized by it. The healthier a marriage, the easier it is to resolve conflict, a true staple in a thriving marriage. As you can see in the diagram, the lower in the phases you move, the closer you get to divorce.

Your marriage can drop from what you think is Thriving to Conflictual because of an event. Lots of secrets have been kept from a spouse only to be revealed, forever changing the relationship.

The Phase system can also be seen as a time line of your marriage. Early in your marriage you may have been thriving, but then an event happened; it took you into Conflictual. But, with therapy and hard work, you have been able to move to Working or maybe even back to Thriving.

This book starts at the bottom of the phase system and works its way up. It has been my experience that no one wants to move to divorce. Even with those spouses who have every legitimate, unselfish reason to do so, they want to avoid it. They want their marriage to work. By starting the book in the lowest point of the system, you can steadily learn what you need to do to make Your Best Marriage.

Chapter 2 – Divorce

"To get divorced because love has died, is like selling your car because it's run out of gas." -Diane Sollee

--

Maybe you are considering divorce. Lots of people do, but are you sure you have tried everything? For many couples, divorce is considered way too quickly and therapy, not quickly enough. It has been said that marriage therapy is like having a hole in your roof. If it's not raining, you don't need a repairman.

Men and women have agonized in my office over the prospect of divorce. Personal safety and the health of the children are at stake. Still, a husband or wife will struggle with the idea of legally removing themselves from the life of their spouse. It is no easy decision.

If you must end your marriage, you want to make sure that you have indeed tried everything. Maybe this book is your last ditch effort to save your relationship. Maybe it is the first step in making your marriage the best it can be.

Where do you start if you are at the point of considering divorce? Your spouse has become your enemy. You simply cannot talk anymore and the thought of speaking to him or her is nauseating. I'm with you. Your spouse vowed to honor, respect and basically treat you right. Remember though, you vowed the very same thing.

I often have my couples, who still, at least a little bit, want to save their marriage, to think about their children. While a child can't save your marriage, he or she is representative or a reminder of the love that brought you together. Motivation for the well-being of your offspring should encourage you to at least try. It is one thing you have in common with your spouse when all other things have failed.

In the movie, The Story of Us, Bruce Willis and Michelle Pfeifer do an excellent job of acting like they love each other when they are around the children. That's the magic of cinema. In real life, your children know when things aren't going well. They can feel the tension in the room and are very adept at diagnosing the mood quicker than a resident from Harvard Medical School. You cannot hide your marriage problems from most children.

Consider the following statistics:

- The poverty rate for a child in a single parent home is six times above that of a married, two-parent home. Typically, the household income of a divorced family falls 37%.1

- Surveys have found that children from broken homes, when they become teenagers, have two to three times more behavioral and psychological problems than do children from intact homes. Zill and Schoenborn, 1988

- Good remarriages did not seem to help children overcome the trauma of divorce. Dr. Judith Wallerstein, The Unexpected Legacy of Divorce, A 25 Year Landmark Study, 2000

- Children living with both biological parents are significantly less likely to suffer health problems than children raised in a single parent home. Dawson. 1991

- Five years after the divorce, one third of fathers see their children very little, if at all.2

- Nearly two-fifths of all kids live in homes without their father. Of those children more than half have never been in their father's home, and 40 percent have not seen them in at least a year. David Blankenhorn, "Fatherless America" 1995

- Daughters, white or black, between the ages of 12 and 16 who lived with unmarried mothers are at least twice as likely to become single parents themselves. McLahan 1988

- Family instability or disruption is one of the major causes of youth suicide, now the second leading cause of death among adolescents. Nelson, Furbelow and Litman, 1988

- Children of divorce complain: "The day my parents divorced is the day my childhood ended." Dr. Judith Wallerstein, The Unexpected Legacy of Divorce, A 25 Year Landmark Study, 2000

Certainly a bad marriage can be harmful to a child, but if there's any chance the marriage can be salvaged, your child can be helped exponentially. You are showing her that you work on your relationships. You don't just leave when things get tough, or when things don't go your way.

Marriages can end rather quickly. When a couple starts a life together, and they do not foster that relationship, they slowly become enemies rather than friends. How does this happen?

First, couples get tied up in the day-to-day activities and marriage gets put on the back burner. Divorces seem to spike within the range of 4 to 7 years.4 Much is debated as to why but given my observation, I see couples within this range struggle with a lot of things. New kids, an ever growing stress from their job and the idea that "wow, I'm giving up a lot for this person" are some of them. Especially, if you got married at a young age, you are seeing marriage through adult eyes after that first six years. Suddenly the drunken parties aren't as fun when it's your stuff they're breaking. The bar scene is no longer exciting when you have a kid at home. If you do not manage your life together and sacrifice for the other, your growing apart begins.

Second, you think the other person doesn't care for you. Some couples believe they are fine. "Nothing is happening," they tell me. Well, this is a problem because nothing is happening. There are no movements towards affection, joy, or anything that resembles happiness. The two spouses just pass by one another in the hallway like strangers. This lack of activity with one another can lead to an unfulfilling marriage and can cause someone to want to seek affection elsewhere.

Third, you are bored. Routine in a marriage can remove the spark but it doesn't have to be this way. You can make time for one another. Married life is like walking over a hilly plain. The two of you are together early on, but for various reasons, one of you continues over a hill; the other goes on in a different direction. You are still close by, but cannot see one another. This creates a feeling of isolation even though you are close by. You must join on a regular basis through recreational activities, conversation and sex. All three of these must be fulfilling. You have probably lost the feeling of love you once had for your spouse. Rediscover this. Find it in yourself to act and to feel love for your husband or wife.

Are you considering an affair? Do you think that person will be better for you? You may think so, but wouldn't you be better off improving your current marriage? If you start a new relationship, those things that hurt your old marriage can also become evident in your new relationship. Then, you are right back where you started. Work diligently at fixing what you have.

Fourth, stress can also lead your marriage down a distressing path. Stress is a part of this marriage or your next three so why not work on this one? Learn to communicate better; learn to work as a team with your spouse. This is the only way you will make it together.

Finally, you find someone else. When the above three issues are going against your marriage, anyone can seem appealing. They talk to you at work, they are nice, and they seem to enjoy your company. They also have none of the baggage that you signed on for when you got married: kids, bills and responsibilities. This "baggage" can be a good thing if you are handling things right. You can enjoy your kids and the other responsibilities that come with a family or you can loathe them. In any case, when you choose to have a physical or emotional affair with someone, you are choosing to destroy the other life you have built.

The second marriage has a tremendous chance of failure. You must make your current marriage work if there is even the slightest chance you want it to. It is really up to you.

You're never too far-gone in your marriage, if you're willi

make the journey back. When you think you stop m

problems with a divorce, all you really do is trade those

problems for a whole new set and sometimes, your problems

can worsen. You will continue to have marital issues if you

don't resolve bad habits. In addition, you will have your

spouse's family to deal with.

If you must divorce, or if you have and your current marriage is good, then you are doing something right. Sometimes, things do get better because you mature, or you leave a frightfully bad situation. However, this is the exception rather than the rule. Chances are you will leave your marriage hurt, you won't be the best of friends, and finding lasting happiness elsewhere is going to be really difficult.

Dave Willis of Marriage Works Says, "Couples who make it aren't the ones who never had a reason to get divorced; they are simply the ones who decided early on that their commitment to each other was always going to be bigger than their differences and their flaws."

BOOKS

The following books are highly rated on Amazon.

- *Contemplating Divorce: A Step-by-Step Guide to Deciding Whether to Stay or Go* by Susan Gadoua

- *Too Good to Leave, Too Bad to Stay: A Step-by-Step Guide to Help You Decide Whether to Stay In or Get Out of Your Relationship* by Mira Kirshenbaum

- *How to Know If It's Time to Go: A 10-Step Reality Test for Your Marriage* by Dr Lawrence Birnbach

- *One More Try* by Chapman

SOURCES

1. HTTP://www.heritage.org/research/reports/2012/09/marriage-Americas-greatest-weapon-against-child-poverty

2. Arnett, Jeffrey, Emerging Adulthood: The Winding Road from the Late Teens through the Twenties, Oxford, 2004.

3. HTTP://www.fatherhood.org/fatherhood-data-statistics#sthash.AiSDGBz7.puff

4. HTTP://priceonomics.com/when-can-you-expect-to-get-divorced/

Chapter 3 – Conflictual Marriage

*"A good marriage is the union of
two good forgivers."* –Ruth Bell Graham

--

John and Sara argue about everything. I often listen to them and wonder, "What are they arguing about?" Literally, everything is an argument and it is not about big stuff either. They fight about the look she gave him after he did the dishes, about how much time he spends on his phone and it's about who does more of the housework. In our sessions, it is a constant back and fourth contest over who has it worse or better in every aspect of life. I try to make them mad at me just so I can get in on the conversation and do some work . . . but they like me. They do not like each other.

The Conflictual Phase is where most people find themselves when they realize, "Hey, we better start doing something." Is it too late if you find yourself here? I don't think so, but it will require a great deal more work than someone who may find him or herself in a different phase.

First, what brought you here? Was it an event like an affair, or has it been a slow process as the marriage was neglected over the last five, ten or fifteen years? Does your spouse have a bad habit that is harmful to the marriage? I've never had a couple tell me, "I'm so glad my husband/wife drinks all the time. It is so good for us." Bad habits hurt the marriage. You might also be here because of a long endured, detached marriage, and you have just had enough. Whatever the case, you are as close to divorce as you will ever be when in this Phase.

What does a Conflictual marriage look like? It's obviously characterized by conflict as spouses engage in negative interactions more than they do positive. One or both members of the marriage speak contemptuously of one another on a regular basis. According to John Gottman, this is one of the biggest predictors of divorce. Do you speak down to your wife? Do you make fun of your husband and he's not laughing, this is called contempt.

Also, staying together has the potential to harm the children and/or spouse. If there's violence of any sort, separating should be considered at a minimum until help is sought and acquired. However, if you do not work on the marriage in this state, your children will only see a dysfunctional marriage. While they may still pick up on some positive attributes, the dysfunction is the major characteristic modeled for the children. A functional marriage works for all involved while a dysfunctional family does not help the individuals reach their brightest potential.

It would be impossible for me to say all that there is on what makes a Conflictual marriage (or any marriage for that matter) but here are some distinct qualities a conflictual marriage will have.

- Time is spent together out of obligation and to keep a sense of normalcy for the children.

- Because you think it will harm the children, you are afraid of leaving your spouse. It very well may but in a conflictual marriage, staying together can do as much, if not more harm.

- Spouses do not feel loved, respected or appreciated. There may be glimmers, but in general you do not feel anything that resembles a good relationship overall.

- You discuss divorce with your spouse or with a friend. You have tried everything (or nothing) at this point, and you think the only way out is to end it.

- One or both spouses keep a variety of secrets. People, who have nothing to hide, hide nothing. If there are secrets, you have a problem

- A couple in a conflictual marriage will exhibit emotional and physical symptoms such as anxiety and depression.

- Interactions between the spouses are characterized by anger.

- Communication about anything other than the simplest of subjects ends up in an argument.

- Interactions can be characterized by selfishness. At least one spouse wants only what he/she wants and doesn't consider the other person.

You are never too far-gone if you're willing to make the journey back. However, some scars may be too deep to heal; only you can decide this. Has she been unfaithful? Has he said he will change and has yet to accomplish this for a time longer than two weeks? There comes a point when you must throw in the towel; only you can decide the timing.

You are considering divorce at this point because staying together has the potential to harm the children and/or yourself. However, divorcing has its own set of problems. You may be getting out of a difficult marriage, but now you are moving into an unknown situation. If you are already dating, then you are about to see what being married to this person is like. Or, if you aren't dating, you are about to see how difficult life can be alone. Perhaps, in your situation, things will get better; hopefully so.

Also, your spouse may not be the best example to your children but he/she is your child's parent and that means something. I have worked with countless children who are with their custodial parent, but they want desperately to be with the parent that isn't in their lives. Who chooses to not be in their child's life and who shouldn't be? The parent simply is bad for the child; the parent's rights have been severely limited. Before moving to divorce, think long and hard about the outcome your spouse has on your child.

This is a crucial point as you must answer this question, "Do the benefits of staying together outweigh the benefits of divorcing?" Or "Is the cost of either worth the trouble?" Whatever you choose, there will be consequences. Which choice can you live with?

HOW TO MOVE OUT OF THE CONFLICTUAL MARRIAGE

Your first option is to divorce. Depending on your personal convictions regarding this topic, the decision might be easy or extremely difficult. However, if you want to work on the marriage, here's what I suggest.

First, find a trained counselor. This is non-negotiable. Look for a marriage counselor whose values are very close to your own. If he or she is not even close to being a Christian and you want Christian counseling, you may not work well with this person. Good counselors are able to connect with the values of the individuals that come to them, but they are only human. Their values can influence how well they work with you. Also, you must like the counselor. How well you get along with him or her is a big predictor in counseling success. A quick Google search will you find many counselors in your area. Many have blogs and ebook pages and with a quick look you can see if this is someone you could have coffee with or invite to your family's barbecue. Not literally of course, but this is the amount of trust and comfort you want with your counselor. If he or she is too weird for you (we are an enigmatic bunch), then you probably won't get along.

Second, I recommend the following books to help you learn how to do what happy couples do. This is often the problem. Unhappy couples are such because they do unhappy couples things like never spending time together, filling this time with yelling. You must learn better habits if you are to have a better marriage.

What is different in a conflictual marriage more than any of the others? The heart is hurt or it's been hardened against the one you are supposed to love, and to fix it much work must be done. For this I recommend the following:

BOOKS

- *Love and War: Find Your Way to Something Beautiful in Your Marriage* by John and Stasi Eldredge

- *One More Try: What to do When Your Marriage is Falling Apart* by Gary Chapman

Our young men are not being taught proper etiquette and manners for interacting with girls. They grow up not knowing

20

how to treat women which results in wives wondering wh
married such morons. If you are a man and are having a
time understanding yourself and your wife, I recommend the
following books.

- *Wild at Heart: Discovering the Secret of A Man's Soul*
  by John Eldredge

- *The Journal of Best Practices* by David Finch

For the ladies, learn to understand yourself and your man. For
this, I recommend the following:

- *When A Woman Inspires Her Husband:
  Understanding and Affirming the Man In Your Life*
  by Cindi McMenamin

- *Captivating: Unveiling the Mystery of A Woman's
  Soul* by John and Stasi Eldredge

Finally, your counselor may recommend a marriage intensive. I
typically do when I believe the couple's boulder of destruction is
racing down the hill faster than I can catch it. A marriage
intensive is a multi-day program that can give your marriage the
shot in the arm it needs. These are intensives I'm familiar with.
Do a Google search in your area for "Marriage Intensive."

- **Your Best Marriage** / www.DaleSadler.net

- **Family Dynamics Institute** / www.familydynamics.net
  "A New Beginning" - Nash, TN 3/28-3/30

- **Marriage Helper** / www.marriagehelper.com
  March 14-16 or 28-30

Chapter 4 – Detached Marriage

"Chains do not hold a marriage together. It is threads, hundreds of tiny threads which sew people together through the years."
-Simone Signoret

--

The Detached Marriage is characterized by not doing anything to strengthen the relationship. Once thriving, you settled into a pattern of working, and since your emotional connection has not been cultivated, detachment occurs. Nothing is really happening; this is part of the problem. Nothing is happening. The husband and wife handle daily tasks. But even with extra time, they do not choose to spend time together. As you spend no time with one another, a small seed of animosity is planted. This seed grows and grows which leads you to the Conflictual Phase.

In a detached marriage positive interactions happen, but they are infrequent. When the couple isn't stressed and all external factors are going well, they can enjoy one another. However, when things are not going well, the marriage becomes very conflictual. The kids are acting up, money issues, and job problems are just a few of the things that can cause a couple to move from loving one another to blaming one another for everything that is going wrong.

In a working marriage, the spouses are business partners. In a detached marriage, the spouses are roommates. Spouses think they are loved, but speak often of not knowing if the other partner actual does love them. In a detached marriage, routine comes before romance and attempts at romance are made, but they often miss the mark. Because the couple isn't connecting regularly, he doesn't know what candy she likes because they never discuss it.; she isn't interested in sex, because he's not romantic; and he's not romantic because she's not interested in sex. If a thriving marriage perpetuates itself with the good couples do, a detached marriage continues because all the negativity is maintained.

In detached marriages, spouses don't know how to relate to one another. As women have worked so hard to get equality with men, they have lost something along the way. Men don't know how to relate to the women in their lives.

Spouses will argue over the marriage and what is or is not happening. They will also argue over parenting. If there is one element that couples must be together on, it is parenting. I have suggested some books in this chapter to get you on the same page.

Detached couples enjoy activities together, but the activities have nothing to do with their marriage. Although spending time with friends or with their kids, there is always this underlying feeling of detachment. Spouses busy themselves with other things so as to avoid their homes. How awful. The home should be a place of refuge where everyone feels loved but this is not the case. The husband will say, "I need to work in my shop.", or the wife will stay extra long at work to avoid the very people she should be wanting to spend time with.

NOT INTERESTED

The wife asks, "What do you think about this?" The husband responds, "it doesn't matter to me." The husband asks the wife, "what would you like to do?" and she responds, "it doesn't matter."

This open ended back and forth is in an all too familiar one for most couples. It seems like a reasonable dynamic to carry for most people. By relinquishing your option to choose and deferring to your spouse, you are communicating that you care about them and want them to have their way. This certainly sounds like a servant's mindset, but it can sometimes come from a different region of the heart.

I want my wife to be happy so I let her choose the restaurants, where we vacation and often, the clothing I buy. However, when we discuss important issues like church, money and parenting, I always have an opinion. For my friends, this isn't a stretch, but if I am to be invested in my marriage, I must have an opinion on the things that matter to its success. Outback vs Ryan's is a no-brainier; I'll let her pick.. But if it's a matter of our family's success, I must participate. Saying you don't care about important components of your relationship only communicates an apathetic attitude. Don't have an opinion? Work to get one. Your spouse wants you to participate. He or she needs you to participate. To use a lifeboat illustration: If only one of you is rowing, the other must not care much about where you're headed.

REDISCOVER IT

I mentioned in chapter 2 that you probably have lost the feeling of love you once had for your spouse. Rediscover this. Find it in you to act and feel love for your husband or wife. An early reader of this manuscript said, I want to know how to "rediscover it."

If you are floating in the ocean of divorce and very close to leaving your spouse, you must consider the idea that, "Yes, we can have what we had before." Are your values still aligned for the most part? Do you want the same things out of life? If you answered, yes, then you have the ingredients to find the feeling of love again.

Perhaps you have nursed animosity and bitterness rather than love, which has brought you to the point you are now. You know all the ways to hurt your spouse, but you have forgotten how to build them up. To quote Yoda, "You must unlearn what you have learned." New thoughts must precede new habits and then develop into new feelings. A minister friend of mine, Keith Parker, once said, "You'll never feel your way to better actions, but you can act your way to better feelings."

Our society is enamored with the idea of new love, which is actually infatuation. It is indeed powerful, but have you considered that it is powerful in order to establish a strong foundation for true love and commitment? We are less excited about the prospect of seeing one another at our worst, but if you do this correctly, you can encourage the best in your spouse and see that on a regular basis.

After you have decided that the ingredients are there to reestablish love, you must start looking at exactly what things to plant. After reading Gary Chapman's, 5 Love Languages, one couple saw an immediate return on their actions. After deciding to listen to what his wife actually needed, one husband saw a happy wife; something he hadn't seen in a long time. Both started noticing a change in each other.

What does your spouse like? What does he or she not like? Make a decision to act on that. I drink Gatorade after I mow the lawn, I stretch after I exercise, and if my wife has had a tough day, I'll rub her feet. You know what is needed in so many areas of your life. Know what your spouse needs, so be the source to work towards letting her know you care.

It won't be perfect. There will be bumps in the road as you work to rediscover what you have forgotten, but keep working at it. You'll rediscover what your marriage has been missing.

OTHER CHARACTERISTICS OF A DETACHED MARRIAGE

- Relationships are attended outside the marriage that have a negative or potentially negative impact on the marriage.

- The job of one or both spouses is hurting the marriage.

- Interactions between the spouses are characterized by avoidance and apathy but not anger.

- Deep communication is rare and each spouse doesn't think their partner really knows him or her.

- A marriage that is detached can be maintained long term, but more so out of obligation than love. If one spouse has an opportunity to have an affair or leave the marriage, he or she will be greatly tempted.

MARRIAGE BOOKS

- *Becoming Your Spouse's Better Half* by Rick Johnson

- *Fall in Love, Stay in Love* By Willard F. Harley

PARENTING BOOKS

- *Generations to Come: Becoming All Things to Your Child* by Dale Sadler

- *How Children Raise Parents: The Art of Listening to Your Family* by Dan B. Allendar

- *Boys Adrift: The Five Factors Driving the Growing Epidemic of Unmotivated Boys and Underachieving Your Men* by Leonard Sax

- *Girls on the Edge: The Four Factors Driving the New Crisis for Girls* by Leonard Sax

- *Five Love Languages* by Gary Chapman

If you are going to strengthen your marriage, you must take every opportunity to make it what it can be. Subscribe to podcasts like Focus on the Family, follow Marriage Helpers on Twitter or Facebook and get a steady stream of positive marriage information coming in constantly.

The detached phase is where a counselor should be considered. You might work your way to a better marriage but some external guidance can be helpful. Your minister could be of tremendous help, or possibly some close friends. Intensives mentioned in the previous chapter can also be helpful.

Chapter 5 – Working Marriage

"Our greatest weakness lies in giving up. The most certain way to succeed is always to try just one more time." -Thomas Edison

--

A working marriage is where most people find themselves as the years progress. Jobs are more demanding and the children can be very exhausting. So, as husband and wife, you move into business model mode. Are the bills paid? Is the house clean? Are the kids getting to their practices on time? These elements of a person's life can become all consuming. Don't misunderstand me, they are fulfilling. After all, who doesn't love a clean house and mature kids? However, while you tend to all theses elements of your life as CEW (Chief Executive Wife) and CFH (Chief Financial Husband) your spirit is not getting nourished.

Your spouse made your heart flutter early on, but if you are only worried about a balanced checkbook and happy children, your marriage may be working but it won't be for long. You must look at your spouse and feel something. In a working marriage, you may not. In this working marriage, spouses believe they are loved, but it's not often reciprocal. Romance is infrequent, if it happens at all. Couples enjoy activities, but they have less to do with each other and more to do with kids, church, jobs, etc.

What separates the working marriage from the thriving marriage? It is the feeling you get when you are together. You must spend time together nourishing the relationship. This involves alone time, without the kids doing things that you both enjoy. It can be something as simple as drinking coffee together. My wife and I have done this for years. Most mornings, we get up, watch the news and sip coffee together. This gives us time to reflect on what is happening in our lives and how we can connect. I know what she is feeling and vice versa. We discuss our dreams, frustrations and disappointments on a regular basis for as little as 20 minutes. Sometimes longer, if I'm lucky.

You must have your own activities that you enjoy. Maybe your wife likes to read and you like to hunt. If this is the case, do those things. They contribute to who you are as individuals. However, what do you do as a couple? What is your couple culture? You must have something that you participant in regularly together? Dates aren't always feasible and weekend getaways become expensive after a while. So, how are you maintaining that feeling of love between those things?

It's during these times that you will discuss the family budget, the upcoming calendar and why you love each other.

How well do you recover from conflict? Those in a working marriage handle conflict well, but one of their coping skills is they just forget about it. There's not enough time to discuss it, or they discuss things in a destructive way. Conflict can be good for your marriage, but when it arises, do you return to normal soon thereafter?

MOVE TO THRIVING

You may dip into this area from thriving, or climb into this area from detached. In either case, a working marriage is a good marriage. You have healthy relationships that are complimentary to the marriage. You both still know you are loved. You also know things could be better, but "there just isn't enough time." You put time into what you value most; I know you value your marriage. It is why you do most of what you are doing. You married, had a child and have built a life. If you don't maintain those things, you'll feel like a failure. True enough, but what if your marriage fails? All that you have built together will come crashing down.

There must be balance here. You are trying to live that type of life but do you continually push your marital needs and your personal needs to the side? If so, after a while, there will be nothing there to give the children. The best thing you can give them is an example of a thriving marriage.

Here are 12 Things Happy Couples do Everyday from the Huffington Post.

1. They have nice, long hugs.

2. They give each other space.

3. They go out of their way for each other without keeping score.

4. They listen.

5. They act silly together.

6. They get serious when they need to be.

7. They make a point to check in throughout the day.

8. They remind each other that love – and staying in love – is a choice.

9. They find ways to brighten each others day.

10. They create their own daily rituals.

11. They cuddle.

12. They slow down together.

Your working marriage is working, but it can be better. Improve some of your good habits in order to have a thriving marriage. Move on to the next chapter and see what must be done.

BOOKS

- *28 Days to A Better Marriage* by Dale Sadler

- *Rescuing Your Love Life: Changing the 8 Dumb Attitudes and Behaviors that Will Sink Your Marriage* by Cloud and Townsend

- *The 5 Love Languages: Secret to Love that Lasts* by Gary Chapman

Chapter 6 – Thriving Marriage

"My wife tells me that if I ever decide to leave,
she is coming with me." -Jon Bon Jovi

--

THE MARRIAGE COMES FIRST

If dysfunction is defined as a system wherein members of the family do not benefit, a thriving marriage can be labeled a family unit where all members benefit greatly. There is open communication and a desire to be together regularly.

In a thriving relationship, spouses feel loved, appreciated, and respected. The children know they are loved, and they know the parents love one another. Regular romance, along with enjoying activities together with the children, will optimize the relationship.

There is a healthy separation between the parental jobs and the marital responsibilities. If one spouse is unable to do something, the other takes up the slack in the best way he or she can. There really is no such thing as "that's your job" so I'm not doing it. Instead, both spouses make the best decision to move forward in the day or week. Certainly, there are jobs that only one spouse will do. This is called sharing responsibilities. But if one must take over because of illness or some other distraction, resentment is not present. There is a mutual respect between the spouses. The wife who is suddenly performing a chore she dislikes is doing so happily because the husband can't perform the chore at this moment. No bitterness occurs because the husband will be grateful and gladly performs her chores when the time comes with just as much gusto as he can muster.

This equation works because each spouse has a servant attitude. Each spouse has the best interests of the other in mind. They each know that nothing will be done that isn't necessary or beneficial in someway for the entire family. Even leisure time is beneficial. My wife gets massages and I go fishing regularly. Both are good for us and for the entire family. If we do not care for ourselves, how can we care for each other? How can we be good parents?

A thriving marriage puts nothing before it. Not jobs, not hobbies and not even kids come before the marriage. These items have their place and are healthy, but if you work too much, if you play too much and if your child is your best friend, you cannot have a thriving marriage. Your spouse comes first. His needs are more important than your own and her needs come before yours.

Both of you working together for the betterment of the family unit will prove that you are thriving.

OUTSIDE RELATIONSHIPS

Another thing that can keep a marriage happy and healthy are the complimentary relationships a couple has outside the home. Look at your friends. Do they make you a better man, husband and father? Do your friends constantly bash their husbands causing you to frequently nitpick your husband's flaws? Proverbs 12:26 says, "The righteous is a guide to his neighbor, But the way of the wicked leads them astray."

Be honest. Are you friends good for your marriage? Proverbs 22:24 & 25 say, "Do not associate with a man given to anger; or go with a hot-tempered man, or you will learn his ways and find a snare for yourself." As much fun as you have had with this friend or group of friends, you must not choose them over your spouse. I won't tell you that you must leave them right now, but if they are influencing you away from your spouse, you will need to make a choice.

Take stock. Do your friends have healthy marriages? Do those you have personal relationships with have healthy marriages or at least a healthy idea about what it is to be a man or a woman. To be successful you must surround yourself with successful people. This includes your marriage. If your marriage is strong, work to mentor another couple. A young man who is struggling needs to be called a jerk if that's what you see him as being. A wife who is being selfish needs to be told she's not putting her family first. As Kramer said, maybe you are the "straw that stirs the drink." Maybe you are who others look to as a model marriage. Be that couple.

MAINTAINING A THRIVING MARRIAGE

A thriving marriage doesn't happen because a couple is newly married. I can like just about anybody if I just met them. In a marriage, you both like each other as you start your new life together. However, as you learn new and unexciting things about each other, will you grow together or apart? Will your behavior adapt or continue to drive you away?

A thriving marriage does not happen by accident and it doesn't continue to happen without purposeful decisions. As a couples' life changes (IE. job, children, etc) they must adapt to the situation and not lose sight of the importance of their relationship.

Take a look at what you are doing that is good for your marriage. Keep doing those things. A thriving marriage is made up of good habits that feed the needs of all involved. Don't let selfishness creep in.

RESOURCES

Even if you're in a thriving marriage, read the books I've recommended. They will help you stay away from bad habits that cause marriages to crumble; they will help you strengthen the skills and habits that brought you here. If you find yourself at this level, maybe you need to make a commitment (time and resources allowing) to help other marriages.

Your church is a good place to start a family ministry. We often think of the youth but with marriages crumbling within a congregation's very walls, something must be done. First, I would suggest reading The Marriage Friendly Church by Danny Camp. Believe it or not, your church can be detrimental to your marriage. The activities that often come with a vibrant church put more responsibility on already strained families. The sails of the church will soon fall flat once your families become too exhausted to attend everything that's been planned in an already overflowing calendar. Danny's book will help you consider how your church helps or hurts marriages.

A good men's ministry and active ladies groups are also good components to have. What does it mean to be a good man? What does it mean to be a good woman? Stop quoting Ephesians 5 all the time and actually show what this beautiful chapter looks like. What does honoring look like? What does loving look like on a daily basis. Your men and women need this direction. They are starving for it.

Finally, your marriages need a regular diet of quality lessons. A gospel meeting, class or weekend retreat that focuses on marriage can do wonders for your families. These activities must happen at least every two years. The congregation where I serve as the youth minister, we schedule a couples retreat every two years, and our men regularly do things together. Our ladies also have their WEW group (Women Edifying Women). I wouldn't formalize any of these except to say that we enjoy being together. We are all leading and challenging each other to be better for our families every time we meet.

PART 2

--

Tactics for Marriage Improvement

Part 2 – Introduction

"Many marriages would be better if the husband and the wife clearly understood that they are on the same side." -Zig Ziglar

—

Willard Harley has his 10 emotional needs, Gary Smalley has his five love languages and now Sadler has his 3 fundamentals. I call the following chapters fundamentals because, as my good friend Jackson put it, "marriage books and seminars are always about communication, money and something the man has done wrong." Well, he's right about the first two.

Most people understand what they need to do, they just don't know how. So, it takes guidance from a counselor or a mentor to help direct couples to a better marriage.

I have a client who says she knows what must be done, but she doesn't know how to do it. Crying, she desperately wants to know how she can be a better wife and mother. Her lack of knowledge may be because of a poor example growing up. Despite her shortcomings, she has a strong desire to do better; this will make the difference in her marriage and in yours.

Most everyone knows that to have a better marriage, they need to communicate and ,to think of the other person first, but this is difficult. You know you need to be on the same page about parenting but it's, just not happening.

The following chapters on communication, selfishness and parenting are vital areas in your marriage that you must be honest about. These chapters are not replacements for the books I have listed elsewhere. I respect those who have written complete books on these various topics. Please, seek their further advice.

I have had reluctant spouses come into my office and have an "I knew that" moment when I mention they have to learn to communicate better. Jim Rohn, a motivational speaker, once said, "Success is neither magical nor mysterious. Success is the natural consequence of consistently applying the basic fundamentals." Communicating, thinking of the other person first and working together to raise your family are the fundamentals of marriage that can never be overlooked. By getting these things right, you are setting yourself up for a successful relationship.

Your marriage is in turmoil because you made a big mistake that betrayed trust; you have neglected the marriage for a long time or both. Now, do you want to fight for it? Do you really want a better marriage? If so, be serious about getting better in these areas.

If you master these fundamentals, what will you have? You'll have the marriage you want. You won't be without struggles or hard times, but a general feeling of joy will be a regular part of your life. You'll have great sex that includes both physical and emotional satisfaction. You'll be at peace because home won't be a war zone you dread, but rather it'll be a place of harmony. Your spouse is happy to see you, your children relish your presence, and you come to know the love of Christ through this experience.

Do you really love your spouse? Do you really want to make this relationship work? If all you feel is bitterness towards your spouse, why? Decide that you are going to be the spouse your loved one needs and master the following chapters.

Chapter 7 – Communication

"Ultimately the bond of all companionship, whether in marriage or in friendship, is conversation." -Oscar Wilde

—

Communication is probably the biggest cliche when discussing marital improvement, but it is such because it is so needed. Indeed, the words you say and how you say them make a huge difference. Proverbs 16:24 says, "Pleasant words are a honeycomb, sweet to the soul and healing to the bones." Has your spouse ever told you, "It's not what you're saying, it's how you say it."

What's keeping you from communicating better with your spouse? There was a time when you put all you had into talking. Now, you seem to disagree about everything, if you talk at all. Many couples lack the skill set to communicate effectively, but

49

more than knowing the words to use, we must know how to speak. Matthew 12:34b says, "For the mouth speaks out of that which fills the heart." Before you know what words to speak, you must work on your heart.

Our English language, despite its shortcomings, has an abundance of nuances in tone, volume and word choice. Furthermore, the feelings we have that bring forth our words project onto those with whom we communicate. We can typically hide an angry spirit in order to get along in public. After a bad day, you don't want to be short with someone at church, but we don't hesitate to lash out at our spouses. They know us too well, it is nearly impossible to hide our true feelings from them. If you are angry with your husband or wife, it will not be difficult to spot and thus begins an argument.

You can speak with a counselor who can tell you all about "I" messages and listening, but even those tactics won't overcome a hardened heart. Proverbs 28:14 says, "How blessed is the man who fears always . . . ." What should you be afraid of in a marriage? You should be afraid of losing your husband. You should be afraid of disappointing your wife. The work you do everyday should be work and effort to keep the other happy with you. You'll mess up at times, but don't spend every night playing video games and wonder why you're not a happier couple. Don't curse each other and sleep in separate beds, and then wonder why your marriage isn't better. The answer to your best marriage is right in front of you. Act like you love each other and you will.

"But I don't feel love". Well, I don't care what you feel. An[y] that has made poor marriage decisions over any length of isn't going to feel anything but bitterness. As Bob Newhart said in his famous counseling sketch, "Stop it!" (Look it up on YouTube.)

The rest of Proverbs 28:14 says "but he who hardens his heart will fall into calamity." To become closer to your spouse, your heart must soften. His needs and her needs should come before your own. When you meet your spouses, your needs will be met. Stop with your hard heart and work together. Work to listen and to be the spouse your spouse needs.

This sounds simple but spouses want to feel safe when they communicate. A lack of communication is sometimes the result of a husband or wife who is too scared to speak. Most people wouldn't hit their loved one, but many would use unkind words and in so doing they create an unsafe atmosphere for conversation. So, no discussion happens at all. This eventually leads to communication that is destructive, which eventually leads to a defensive wall. "I'm tired of getting hurt. So, I refuse to let you in anymore."

No one wants to feel fear when speaking to a loved one. We all want to feel safe, and it takes both spouses to make this happen. You must hold up your end of the marriage bargain. Many have built walls out of fear. Help take those walls down by being a source of love and light in your home. Then, loving communication can begin.

WHAT DO YOU TALK ABOUT?

Living with someone can make you complacent in your discussions. You think you know everything about each other, and you think nothing more can be said. The truth is that the longer you live with someone, the less you know. If you don't communicate regularly, conversations with your spouse can be some of the most meaningful discussions you will ever have. So what do two people who know everything about each other talk about?

First, you should be talking about your day. This is generally different for both men and women. Women want to talk about their experiences and be validated for their frustrations and applauded for their successes. Men, we also like to tell our wives about our day but sometimes, we'd just rather forget about it. When I open up about a bad experience from the day, I feel like I'm reliving it. not good. Eventually, we may discuss the bad day we had, but not until we've dealt with it ourselves.

By engaging in this conversation with your spouse, you tell him or her that you care. Their lives are more important to you than anything on television; you are interested in them. I don't always understand what my wife is talking about when she discusses her day at school, but I ask questions and let her know that interested. If you are not interested in your spouse, you need learn to be.

It is vital to your success on this planet, and it is up to each of us to care for the other.

Second, talk about your plans. What are you looking forward to right now with your spouse? Anything? Nothing? You aren't looking forward to sex tonight? You aren't looking forward to a weekend date, a vacation or even something as small as spooning in the bed? You need something in the short-term to look forward to that fills your heart with joy because of your spouse. If not, why not? Find those things that you enjoy with your spouse and do them together. How do you accomplish this? You communicate.

Finally, you and your spouse should talk about long-term goals. Where are you going to be in five, ten or twenty years. If you are working together, you both have something to anticipate; you both work for each other. You are better together than you are apart.

Talk about it.

WHERE IS YOUR COMMUNICATION?

I love theme parks. I have ridden the country's oldest wooden roller coaster, and I have ridden the country's fastest wooden roller coaster. I have eaten churros, fried Oreo and my fair share of turkey legs. I know my way around these bastions of family fun. What is one thing most of them have in common? They all have some type of theme and within that theme are different areas. The Magic Kingdom has Tomorrow Land, Holiday World has Christmas Land and even Dollywood has mining areas and a main street area.

Your marriage's communication can find itself in different areas. Some are lots of fun and others you'd just rather avoid; kind of like Dino Land in Disney's Animal Kingdom. I have designated three different areas a marriage can communicate in. Where is yours?

The first area is anger. You're mad at your spouse or you're mad at someone at work, or you're mad at your child; you take it out on your spouse. Anger is such an easy emotion. If we don't like something, anger is the first tool that many pull out of their pockets. Anger is primal and is a quick attempt to make someone (or something) meet our needs. Many haven't figured it out yet, but yelling at the computer won't make it run faster or do what you want.

I have discussed already how anger is a secondary emotion. You are working to express something underneath your anger. It's why some people say, "I'm not mad, I'm just hurt." The situation of an offending spouse in some way is too much to get angry about so people revert to their actual emotion. This can be very constructive.

The next area we talk about in our marriages is serious talk. "Did you pay the bills? Did you remember to pick up the kids? What's for dinner tonight?" We engage in these conversations constantly; it is what makes up our day. The bridge from point A to point B. Anger can tear this bridge down, or the next area can keep it together.

Finally, we speak in the area of caring. Many couples are in this area in different ways. Many "pick at each other." We kid because we love, correct? This is going on throughout the day and it communicates a sense of affection.

If you don't know what area you are in, it's helpful to "check-in" with your spouse occasionally. Normally, you can tell how he or she lays their stuff down after a day at work. It is important to strive to understand your spouse. Don't assume everything is okay. We never know what's going on inside one another's head, so it's always important to check in.

Chapter 8 – Selfishness

"Marriage, like a submarine, is only safe if you get all the way inside." -
Frank Pittman

———

Conflict in a marriage has many sources. Most say it's money. Others say that even if you get that figured out and can't communicate, you'll fight about something else. I agree. Children are also a point of contention. How we relate to our in-laws, hobbies and our jobs can turn us against our spouses, the person we should be closest to. It can be tough figuring out what you're arguing about because one thing often leads to another. Then, you don't know what to do; you're just mad.

As I observe the above conflicts in my office, many can be boiled down to both spouses wanting something from the other. A recipe for disaster, they are each asking yet not receiving. Neither is willing to give because of selfishness or bitterness, and we are supposed to get something good out of marriage. How can this be fixed?

Each spouse needs to put the family's needs above his or her own. You are after all a partnership. Without this dynamic in place, you'll be on the same team, but working towards different goals. You'll take more time at work, because it's what you want to do. You'll begin buying things because it's what you want. You'll speak with no regard towards the others feelings. One or both of you have become a force in the home not for peace and productivity, but rather for your own agenda.

Does Mark 10:8 not say that you shall become one flesh? More than a metaphor, this is a plan for your life. You each must do what is best for the other. If you get preoccupied with what you want with no regard for the other, your marriage will not function optimally. Never has God in His wisdom through the Holy Spirit writers or through Jesus the Son, advocated looking for one's personal interest.

"But he never thinks of me."; or "But she never does this for me." Indeed, your marriage will never get better if you consistently look at the other and say, "When are you going to start _____?" One of you must take the lead and say, "I'm going to do better."

Jesus never acted in a way that said, "When you act better, I'll help you." He didn't say this to the woman at the well nor to the lepers. Christ looks at us much the same. Your spouse may be struggling with selfishness, pornography, or bitterness but that doesn't mean you have to be the power that keeps them there. Instead, show them the power of Jesus and love them. If you both work towards this end, you'll find your happy marriage.

Think of your marriage as a lifeboat. If you don't work together, you'll be stuck in the ocean; right where you are. Some sit there, waiting on the other to move. Others are doing all the work, and still others paddle in different directions. The worst is when you are both drilling holes in the lifeboat and wonder why you are sinking.

IT'S OKAY TO BE SELFISH?

In marriages, there are givers and there are takers. There's a little of both in all of us, but naturally we may favor one over the other. The trick is to make sure your giving and your taking are in balance. Well, at this point, I'm going to encourage you to be a taker. Take time for yourself and think of yourself more; you can improve your marriage. Ever heard a marriage therapist say that?

First, let me explain this concept further. Think about what you want in your marriage. What do you want it to do for you? Healthy marriages provide for both participants and children can benefit here too. You should be getting something from your marriage. The difficulty begins when you don't know what that something is.

Willard F. Harley Jr. in his book Fall In Love Stay In Love lists ten needs that all people have. What is your top five? (Admiration, affection, conversation, domestic support, family commitment, financial support, honesty and openness, physical attractiveness, recreational companionship and sexual fulfillment) Which are not being met? Which do you need to ask for? Your spouse, if he/she doesn't know, you can't act upon what you need.

For women, let's say they need affection, and men need admiration. (Men, if you don't think it's a need, you are wrong. More on this later.) Now that you've identified a need, consider how you get that need met. Only your spouse can give it. How do you motivate him or her to want to act on your behalf to meet your needs? You've probably said or heard, when you start doing _____, I'll give you what you need. You can't wait for this to happen. Someone must start the process of a good marriage. Who will it be?

A marriage is a reciprocal relationship. If you meet her needs, she'll work to meet yours because she sees that you care and that you're trying. One gives, the next receives, and then is motivated to give.

Next, communicate your needs with your spouse. We become frustrated with our spouse, sometimes for an unknown reason even to us, and conflict begins. More often than not, we are frustrated because a need of ours is not being met. What needs do you have that are not being met? Does your spouse even know what they are?

Third, work on yourself for your marriage. All too often a jaded spouse will point the finger at the other. "If you'd change, things would be so much better", you may say. A wife nags or a husband withdraws and this does not encourage change of any kind from the other. What should you do? Think of yourself and what you need to change. If you want more intimacy in your marriage, be intimate. If you want more honesty in your marriage, be honest. If you want to do more fun things with your spouse, make it happen.

This sounds difficult, and it is, because for a while you will be carrying a lot of the burden. However, as you become the spouse you want to be, your better half will begin becoming the spouse you desire. Find support in trusted friends. Get connected with them and have them pray for you. "For God, who said, 'Light shall shine out of darkness . . . .'" (2 Corinthians 4:6) Someone has to lead the way. Someone has to begin to change. Think of yourself and begin that change today. Lead your family, as Christ would have you lead them.

Fourth, be happy with yourself. Many spouses look to one another for happiness and this is a good source. However, if there are things in your life that you struggle with, your spouse may not be able to overcome what you feel. The answer? Think of yourself and how you can be happy. What do you need to work on? This is typically a spiritual question? By being happy with yourself, you will exude a confidence that your spouse will find both appealing and inspiring.

Chapter 9 – Parenting

"They say it takes a village to raise a child. That may be the case, but the truth is that it takes a lot of solid, stable marriages to create a village." - Diane Sollee

—

"Don't yell at her like that." "You're just babying him." "Let him grow up." These probably sound like the discussions on parenting that you have had with your spouse. These words are nothing more than critiques of a system that is failing your marriage, but also letting your children down.

You and your spouse may be one of the following types of parents. First, are you lenient? A mother or father asks the child to do something, and he doesn't do it. He continues playing his video games; or he doesn't clean his room; or he doesn't do his homework and the only person that this affects is you. It makes you angry. "Why can't I get him to do anything?", you ask. Well, if this sounds like you, you are failing your child.

You are failing to show him how to listen. You are declining to show him how to care for others. I've heard the answers before. He's a strong-willed child and he'll be the boss someday. Maybe, but what are the consequences to the marriage and family now? What kind of boss (and more importantly future spouse) are you teaching him to be?

We think no one should ever feel uncomfortable, but nothing can build character more in a child or adult than to experience something that is unpleasant. It teaches that the world does not cater to your every whim. When you first come into my office, I want to make you comfortable, but then after rapport is built, it is my job as your counselor to make you squirm. When you are doing what is harmful to your marriage, time to get uncomfortable. How parents raise their children is one of the biggest areas of failure.

Parenting isn't easy and in fact it is a war zone. You don't want to be uncomfortable? If you want to be uncomfortable, have an eight year-old sleeping with you, because you won't teach him he's a big boy now. Try being the parent to a 30 year old who still won't do anything because you never taught her the value of hard work. Be uncomfortable now so you can be proud of your child later. It is much easier to raise a boy than it is to fix a man.

If your child is not acting to your specifications, it's time to do something, but is it too late? I've seen some parents battling with a teenager and in many cases it was because the foundation of parental authority wasn't established early on. If she's not doing what you tell her to do at age 5, she won't do it at age 16 either. You have not asserted your dominance in the home, but rather your son or

daughter has most likely asserted theirs. They control the atmosphere and what happens on a day-to-day basis. It may be very difficult , but it is not too late to be a parent.

What should you expect from your child? First, he should listen when you tell him something. He listens because he knows you mean what you say. He listens because it will somehow affect him. He listens because it is understood that you are in charge. I have heard children and teens say, "I win the arguments at our house." Parents, you are losing more than an argument, if this is the case. You must, at any cost, teach your child that you are in charge.

Secondly, a good parent/teen relationship has mutual respect. My daughter knows I will give her a level of respect, and she appreciates this. Who wouldn't? I am firm with my children, but I do not advocate bossing them around. Instead, there are established guidelines that are easily understood. The atmosphere in the home is one of respect and trust.

I tell my son to do the dishes and carry out the garbage. What if one day I suddenly yelled at him, Why isn't this garbage taken out yet?" I just changed the rules on him. This is confusing and upsetting to the child. Why would you do that? Teachers know what I mean when I say that their jobs seem to almost change quarterly. What is expected of them is always on the move; it is extremely frustrating. You must establish patterns in your house that are predictable. If you constantly create new expectations, your child will get frustrated and not listen.

If the established pattern is that you yell at your child to do his homework and he doesn't do it because he's busy snap-chatting, then you have established a pattern that will not work. The pattern should be that all chores are done before any electronics are started.

One of the best movies to watch on parenting is Nanny McPhee. All she does for the weak father who can't control his children, is teach them five lessons.

- To go to bed when they are told.

- To get up when they are told.

- To get dressed when they are told.

- To say please and thank you.

- To Listen

What is the magic in these lessons? There is no magic in the real world, but the principles are the same. A child has a certain degree of power when it comes to bedtime. If a child simply holds out longer than you, he or she will get their way; sleeping with you, or staying up later than normal are two examples. All they have to do is wear you down, and you'll give in. Everyone knows a tired parent is a push over. Also, if the child doesn't get out of bed when he is told, then he is either a heavy sleeper or he is disobeying directions from the parent. And he hasn't even started the day. They don't plot this out, but it's what their behavior shows us.

Lastly, manners should be taught to all children. Please and thank you are but two phrases, yet they translate into big concepts. By saying please, a child understands he cannot simply command someone to obey their will. An important lesson indeed. Second, thank you considers the other person's time, feelings, and commitment to whatever the gratitude was extended. Imagine a boy who never appreciates his mother's cooking. He will not see the value in her work, nor in the future wife he may someday curse with his lack of thoughtfulness.

Another lesson lots of children miss is when is the appropriate time to speak. I have been visibly speaking to a colleague in the hallway at my school when a child just a few feet away begins to get my attention. Was she on fire? Was a lion loose in the building? No. She wanted to speak; she believed she had every right to do so. By teaching a child appropriate times to speak, he or she learns self-control and that their ideas are not to always be considered under any circumstance.

The overwhelming power of Nanny McPhee's lessons are that they have a ripple affect into the rest of an individual's life. They create structure as the parent directs a child's start and end of the day. Consider bed making. Many do not see the purpose in making up a bed to start the day, but commit to doing it for a week and notice how you feel when you see it. There is accomplishment. There is a life lived to such a degree that things can be kept in some semblance of order. Above all else, discipline is in bed making; we need discipline in our entire life.

The discipline required to do a small task such as the making of a bed will have a ripple affect, just like thank you and please. Don't' worry about teaching your son or daughter discipline, make them engage in it through chores or habits that will make discipline happen.

By getting dressed when they are told, you exert a level of control over them that will also extend into other areas of their lives. Can you make a child eat? Can you make a child get dressed? Unless you force the food into their mouths and physically manipulate their bodies to put their clothes on, no. For those who follow the directives of eating and getting dressed (among other things) the parental unit has developed a level of control over the child. Any child can refuse anything the parent asks or tells the child to do. However, a healthy parent/child relationship is one where the parent instructs and the child obeys. If the child thinks he's running things, he won't put his clothes on when told, and he won't follow your guidance when you instruct him in more important ways.

It's the little things that matter.

Chapter 10 – How You Handle Conflict

"It is sometimes essential for a husband and a wife to quarrel – they get to know each other better." -Goethe

—

Imagine coming home, greeting your spouse and within ten minutes the atmosphere is tense. You're not sure what's going on, but you become frustrated. There's any number of things that could be happening. He could be mad about his day but not at you. She could be upset about the day as well, but is now taking it out on you. This is called displacement; being mad at someone or thing and taking it out on someone else. Maybe the feelings being expressed are from an earlier argument. In any case, arguments and tension are a normal part of a marriage, and how you handle these moments are foundation in having a happy marriage.

The normal pattern of these moments occurs like this: An event triggers feelings, which when expressed in a confrontational way by spouse A leads to a response from spouse B. At this point, spouse B holds the key to how this moment will progress. Everyone will get angry and have a bad day on occasion, but then you are at a crossroads. Do you escalate the situation, or do you help your spouse with what is angering them?

A typical reaction is to escalate the situation especially, if your spouse is angry with you. If you are the object of the emotion, then something is not right in the world. What is your reaction? Your reaction should be an apology, if you've done something wrong. If it's the result of something else, it should be sympathy. Other reactions include defensiveness and returning anger with anger.

When you're upset, this is your knee jerk reaction, but now that you are thinking clearly without a conflict, consider what Proverbs 16:21-24 says,

> The wise in heart will be called understanding, and sweetness of speech increases persuasiveness. Understanding is a fountain of life to one who has it, but the discipline of fools is folly. The heart of the wise instructs his mouth and adds persuasiveness to his lips. Pleasant words are a honeycomb, Sweet to the soul and healing to the bones. There is a way which seems right to a man, but its end is the way of death.

When engaging in conflict and viewing anger as an option, you must consider what it is you want out of the situation. Do you think to yourself, "Hmm. I want my wife to get even madder than she is. Let me see how I can make this worse." No one thinks this, but it's often the result of their actions.

People get angry when they want something to be different than it is. They are faced with a situation and because it's not optimal, they resort to a fight response, or at least a disgruntled disposition. Anger is a useful emotion, but many people use it like a multi-tool to change situations and get what they want. Or, they just don't know how else to react. There are other ways.

Don't allow your emotions to rule you. Instead, consider right now what you're going to do in the heat of the moment and react accordingly. Think about each conflict as a moment to work through instead of a battle to win. If you are wrong, apologize. If you believe your spouse is ultimately wrong then reciprocating the anger will not make things better. "You're so stupid." This phrase never works but is often what people want to say. Neither does yelling or becoming defensive against the perceived onslaught on your character. These are all typical reactions.

Instead of the reactions we resort to by default, we must consider more thoughtfully how to react. When I work with couples, I don't try to figure out who did what or why someone else is right. Instead, I try to teach them how to handle conflict constructively. Again, everyone is going to be mad, but not everyone has to resort to ensuring the war continues.

So, we know the first three stages of a conflict: event, anger, expression. Spouse A points expression towards spouse B, who has a choice of escalating or working things out. We already know how to escalate, but to problem solve a new set of skills is necessary.

First, recognize that your spouse is upset. This will be easy to do as he or she has some typical signs of anger. You might want to immediately become frustrated yourself over your perception of an unreasonable reaction to what you think your spouse is angry over. But keep in mind, you're not sure yet, and you could be very wrong. Assumption is a step in the wrong direction. So, give your spouse time to express what they are feeling, or if you're brave, ask. I have found that the direct approach is best. Otherwise, by not asking you communicate that you haven't noticed or don't care. So, ask what's going on and be prepared to listen.

Next, allow your spouse to talk about what's going on. Listen, and don't be too quick to offer suggestions. Wives especially just want to vent about what's going on with them. Men typically just want to forget about it rather than relive it, but talking about it can also bring relief.

As they discuss their feelings, listen for what he or she is trying to say. What feeling is your spouse trying to convey? Are they sad? Are they confused? Are they disappointed? Figure this out and speak to that. "I know you're sad/confused/disappointed and I'm sorry." This will go along way in problem solving the situation. Rarely is the person just angry. Anger is a secondary emotion that is used to express an underlying feeling such as the previous ones mentioned. Men in particular do this. We don't like uncomfortable feelings so we get mad about it.

If your spouse comes to you upset, you're trying to defuse the bomb of anger. By validating his or her feelings, you take a step towards problem-solving. All that's needed right now is an apology, or at least an acknowledgment of the wrong that's been done. Once your spouse has calmed down, effective conflict resolution can begin.

Now, if you are the offended spouse here (the one who is upset), you can also present your thoughts and feelings in a way that either escalates or problem-solves. You are allowed a little more freedom here to be upset. However, this is not a ticket to go full-blown insane, rip up your spouse, or cry about how his or her parents failed. You also have a responsibility to work on problem-solving the situation. How can you help your spouse understand your position? Is your thinking reasonable? If not, this should be where you start the problem solving method. Maybe you have misunderstood your spouse, which is why you're upset. You should start here figuring things out.

How do you problem-solve? This involves understanding and being understood. What does your spouse want? Remember, all people want to be validated and essentially saying to their loved one that their feelings matter. You move closer to a peaceful consensus.

A conflict has occurred and you mustn't put it in the closet to be brought out later. As you recognize your spouse's feelings, you both must now discuss the issue in a constructive way. Work with the end in mind. The best consensus is not what you want, but rather what is best for the goals of the family. If you don't have mutually agreed upon goals, your personal agendas will regularly be in conflict. They'll either be selfish or have the whole family in mind. If not agreed upon, you're like two people rowing a canoe in two different directions.

- **Problem Solve**
  - Work to understand your spouse
  - Work to be understood
- **Validate**
  - Your spouse's feelings matter
  - Discuss the issue at hand
- **Reconcile**
  - Apologize and forgive
  - Adapt behavior for future to reduce conflict
- **Consensus**
  - Work towards a win-win situation
  - What is best for the family

How else can you handle conflict? It's a rare thing, but my wife and I have actually just gone to bed. We aren't mad, but a lot of times the things we argue about are because we are tired. If the issue isn't important, work to forget about it. Is the way your spouse folds towels really important? If it is, talk about it when you aren't angry.

Chapter 11 – Where is God in Your Marriage?

"Many are the sorrows of the wicked, But he who trusts in the Lord, lovingkindness shall surround him." -Psalm 32:10

—

What I see a lot of in my office are couples who are angry with one another. This anger can be a good thing as the spouses fight to get what they both want: a better marriage. No one fights for something they don't want so I appreciate a frustrated couple. I can take this anger and cultivate it into forward momentum. However, sometimes this anger is so intense that there is no room for love to begin to grow. Spouse A is the cause of all the distress in the marriage (according to spouse B), and spouse B has his or her back against the wall ready to fight. So much anger has developed that a crowbar couldn't pry it open for the smallest seed of affection to take root. Not only that, but I very quickly become another object of the spouse's anger for any number of reasons. These couples definitely need the forgiving power of Jesus.

The spiritual side of our marital relationship is often forgotten, but it is where God's love for His church plays out best in our earthly relationships. Parenting also does this. As we are blessed with children, we catch a glimpse of God's love for us.

After two people marry, things begin to change. Before marriage, you almost always saw the best of the other person, but now you are about to see the worst. What is she like in the morning? How good is he at handling money? What are his/her really annoying habits? You may have seen glimpses of them during courtship, but now you are about to be thrown completely into them. And herein is the beauty of marriage.

We begin to see each other as we are, our faults and our strengths. This does something to each of us. To spouse A, who is now learning a great deal more about spouse B, it is a test of commitment. Are you committed enough to overlook the many shortcomings you will now see in your spouse? Jesus does this for you as he looks past all your sins but loves you anyway. Ephesians 5:28-30 says,

> So husbands ought also to love their own wives as their own bodies. He who loves his own wife loves himself; for no one ever hated his own flesh, but nourishes and cherishes it, just as Christ also does the church, because we are members of His body.

Part of the lesson here is that we ought to love ourselves; many people have difficulty with this. So, here the grace and love of Jesus must first be realized. If your marriage is in trouble, is it because you don't even love yourself? Jesus loves you and by learning to love yourself, you can return that love to others.

WHERE HAVE ALL THE MEN GONE?

For the last several decades, boys have been raised to believe that women are their equals and in many ways they are. However, women are not equal to men; they are far better and more precious creatures than my kind could ever dream of being. They have a natural propensity for caring and nurturing, and possess a superhero level of intuition.

Times have changed. Gone are the days where men smoked cigars while the wife delivered the baby. Thankfully, men take a more active role in their children's lives and this is a good thing. However, sometimes with change come unintended consequences. While boys are being taught that girls are the same, they are losing the message that girls should be treated differently. They should never be harmed; they should be protected, and they should be cherished as the wonderful beings God intended them to be. If God created Adam to tend to the garden, he created Eve to make it beautiful. Certainly, our wives do this today.

Despite a man's more active role in the home, boys are still around women a great deal of their lives. They are around their teachers at school, in Bible class and at home, if dad gets home later than mom. Also, with boys being sheltered and play-time being relegated to video games, restrictions to anything unsafe such as guns, firecrackers, etc., the time and interaction between a father and son grows smaller and smaller.

A boy who doesn't regularly engage with his dad isn't learning what it means to be a man. A single mother can do her best to teach her son how to be a man, but without the example of strong men in his life (coaches, uncles, etc), he may never learn. Instead, what he will learn is that women cater to him. Then, when he is married, he will expect this of his wife who thought she was marrying her knight, her champion. Instead, she's married a boy who expects her to do what all other women in his life have done, care for him. Now, she is extremely frustrated because her husband is nothing more than an additional child.

True manhood has been cast to the sidelines with white-wall tires. However, there are those who want to be all they can be for their family. They push aside modern convention and respectfully lead their household in such a way that the wife adores him and the children admire him. He is strong both in body and conviction. He is authoritative, yet listens. He is soft, yet firm, and when any danger is at the door, he will answer.

Over the last several years, gender equality has been championed as the next great cause to get behind. I am all for equality, but what many don't understand is that while girls are excelling and doing better, boys are falling behind and doing worse. When will this downward spiral of our boys be recognized? Since the 1950s, girls have crawled steadily ahead of boys in the areas of high school and college diploma attainment.[1] The class of 2017 has a huge gap between the genders according to the US Department of Education. Consider the following chart[2]

US College Degrees by Gender

Degrees	Class of 2017			Class of 2026 (est)		
	Male	Female	Females per 100 males	Male	Female	Females per 100 males
Associate's	37.9%	62.1%	164	34.9%	65.1%	187
Bachelor's	42.9%	57.3%	134	41.8%	58.2%	139
Master's	41.7%	58.3%	140	41.6%	58.4%	140
Doctor's	47.8%	52.2%	109	47.6%	52.4%	110
All Degrees	41.5%	58.5%	141	40%	60%	150
Source: US Department of Education						

Our society is "unlearning masculinity." College campuses are full of "women's centers" and "gender equity" initiatives. I'm glad my daughter has a better chance than her great grandmother, but when my son is struggling, needs help and I'm not close by, where will he go?

GOD'S PLAN FOR THE HOME

"Only one in five young men would feel confident tackling a dripping tap. Two thirds of millennial males don't know how to change the oil in their car. And just three in ten men are comfortable with the assembly of flat pack furniture."[3]

In Ephesians 5 we read of God's plan for the marital union. Verses 22 and 23 say that wives are to be subject to their husbands and that the husband is to be the head of wife. This is an organizational system that has been misused in the past and disregarded as old-fashioned in our modern society, but I have seen young wives long for its wisdom time and time again regardless of religious affiliation or upbringing.

After the honeymoon is over, women want the husband to do something; anything. She wants him to have an opinion and move in a way that is beneficial to the family. Sadly, many men don't know what this looks like. If he tries to lead he's called a misogynist. If he does nothing he is called a child.

There was a time when the man being the head of the house meant that the wife did whatever he said regardless of her skills or wisdom on the matter. If he wants to stay out all night and drink, the wife should respect this. Many misguided men have touted this dynamic even within the last ten years. This is wrong by societal standards but it's also unbiblical. While God has designed the home with the man as the head, this by no means gives him the right to live as he pleases.

The home is often divided into roles between the husband and wife. Sometimes these roles are clearly defined and others are more fluid. In general, I see women who know the part they play in the home. They have jobs and care for the children, which typically involves shopping and spending time with them. Pretty much everything else is divided between the husband and wife, at least in theory.

The men I see who are struggling in their marriages have less of a defined idea about what they are supposed to do. Remember, the women in their lives have always cared for them. The conflicts I see a lot of are the women asking the man to do something. Whether it's sharing in the household chores, spending more time with her and the kids or not playing video games all the time, this is a typical point of contention. What is the man actually doing? The wife is doing a lot already. She has a natural inclination to care for a home and those inside it. A man's natural inclination has been stifled by our modern society. Men are still wild animals and teaching them how to use this characteristic in their lives is vital to their survival.

Men are leaders, naturally decisive, and protectors. Now, typically one would need to ask forgiveness of womankind for suggesting that a man can do something (anything) more or better than a woman. I'm not suggesting this at all. I'm simply encouraging men to use their abilities to earn respect in their homes and contribute to the family. I think any wife would be proud if this happened. Men have good qualities that make our families stronger. By their contribution, good men can turn their daughters into confident women and their sons into men of integrity.

In Ephesians 5:22-26 Paul compares the home to Jesus' relationship with the church. He loves it, He died for it and the church is subject to Him. In exactly the same way, the husband loves his wife, would die for her and she is subject to him. It's this last part that any woman born after 1970 cringes at, but let me ask some questions of the wives. What do you want your husband to do? Do you want him to be that second or third child? Do you want him to lie around and do nothing or do you want him to take an active role in the home? He's not the caregiver you are. He's not good at plenty of other things you're good at which might mean handling money or even fixing the car. Being subject to him doesn't mean you are his servant, and it doesn't mean you are inferior. It is an instruction for the husband to take an active role in the home. What does this look like in 21st century America?

He is the protector of the home. This might mean he protects the home from his poor spending habits so you control the checkbook. You look to him for what the family values whether it's your spiritual life, sports or the outdoors. (Or all three.) You of course share these values, but you want him to champion them. You want to communicate what is important to you and you want him to make that happen. He is the coach of the home who wants every member to succeed.

When a man is using his talents for the betterment of the home, women should be using theirs. Ephesians 5:22-24 is about God's deal with man. If something goes wrong in the home, God is going to speak to the man. Who did God call for in Genesis 3? Adam. God through His knowledge knew what had happened and wanted to speak to Adam. Eve had to answer as well, but God looked at Adam first.

Men want to be admired in the home. This is one of the needs discussed in Willard F Harley's book, *Fall In Love Stay In Love*. He believes it to be a high need for men, but many I talk to don't admit that it is. They have been diluted or they are not being honest with themselves. Ask yourself men, "do I want to be admired?" If not, consider this. Don't you want to be Superman flying through the air after having just saved Lois; her looking at you like her champion? Don't you want to be Batman who stands tall because of his principles? Don't you want to be Jason Bourne, an almost immortal man who can handle any situation? Your wife and your children can look at you in this way if you give them something to respect.

A desire for admiration has been my greatest personal motivator to be a good husband and father. I want to be as strong as Superman, as selfless as Batman and as tenacious as Bourne; all tempered with the love of Jesus. Think about the opposite of admiration; disappointment. Do you want your son or daughter to be embarrassed by your actions? Do you want your wife to look elsewhere for her true champion? I hope not. Be the man they need. Your home needs you desperately.

Ephesians 5:21 instructs us to "be subject to one another in the fear of Christ." Both husbands and wives are answerable to one another. Why? Because we live in the "fear of Christ" meaning we love as He taught and lived. Selfishness from the husband or wife isn't a part of the deal.

WHAT'S A WOMAN TO DO?

Many interpret Ephesians 5 as saying the man is the king of the house, but kings are less likely to give their lives for those under their rule. Ephesians 5 tells of a servant leader, much like Jesus' role on this earth.

The rules of engagement have changed so much many boys and girls don't know how to interact with one another. Women can do it themselves. They are strong, willful and can garner the skills to do most anything. Consider this adage and apply it to the home as a whole: *Men don't open the door for a lady because she can't. He opens the door for her because he can.* Gestures like this communicate that she is special and loved.

I chose my wife because she is strong in many ways, which adds value to my life, but I also chose her because I could add value to her. I could have chosen a wife who did everything for me, but I wanted a wife that could be my partner. I already have a mother. I do things for my wife because it communicates love to her and she reciprocates that love. Our roles in the home compliment each other.

SOURCES

1. https://www.washingtonpost.com/news/wonk/wp/2016/01/28/the-serious-reason-boys-do-worse-than-girls/?utm_term=.bca2292aaa96
2. http://www.nationalreview.com/article/447445/feminization-everything-fails-boys-higher-education-gender-gap-heavily-favors-women
3. http://www.telegraph.co.uk/men/thinking-man/millennial-men-have-gone-soft--but-its-not-our-fault/

Chapter 12 – Affairs and Infidelity

"Love never gives up, never loses faith, is always hopeful, and endures through every circumstance." -I Corinthians 13:7

—

Men and women have innocent relationships outside their marriage. They eat lunch with one another in the break room; they interact personally, and they even talk on the phone every day as part of business relationships. Just because a woman talks to a man, does not necessarily mean something is going on. However, many emotional and physical affairs begin this way, simple interaction fostered an affair.

How can you tell you are on the verge, or already deeply immersed in an emotional affair? If you answer yes to any of these questions, (or if you have the least bit of hesitation) you may be in danger.

- Could you tell your spouse about your conversations without hiding any facts?

- Could your spouse be in the room as a non-participant or participant in your conversation?

- Does the person stand unusually close to you?

- Do you call him/her when you are alone?

- Do you delete his/her text messages regularly?

- Is your relationship seriously based on anything other than business?

How can you stay out of an emotional affair?

- Watch for the above signals.

- Tell your spouse anyone you feel is making advances towards you.

- Always keep conversation on business matters or on the surface regarding personal issues.

- Don't say anything or do anything that should be reserved for your spouse.

Affairs can start anywhere, not just work. If you have a relationship with a person, and you must make an effort to see them, stop kidding yourself. It's an affair.

PHYSICAL AFFAIRS

Defining what is a safe relationship with someone who is not your spouse is quite blurred by some. "It's not an affair if there's no sex." "We only kissed once." "We were just talking." Healthy relationships can occur between members of the opposite sex who are not married, but when that relationship begins meeting needs that only your spouse should meet, a definite boundary has been broken.

Obviously, this means sex, but it also means emotional needs and anything else that is important to you. Your need for social interaction with someone or your need for admiration are some examples. All of the elements mentioned here are crucial to a marriage, and if they're getting met elsewhere, the bond you pledged is in jeopardy.

That coworker you've been spending more time with is starting to do something for you. You begin feeling something you've not felt for your spouse in a long time. You can call it a fire or a spark, but it is also a sign of danger. While your marriage might not be all that you wish right now, having an affair will begin a very painful process. Do you want to go through that? Do you want to put your children through that?

The issues you struggle with in your current marriage can and very well may resurface in subsequent relationships. Plus, an affair is easy to maintain in terms of a relationship. There are no bills, and you only see one another a few times a week so the best impression is always seen. If an affair is followed through to its logical conclusion, what do you have? A spouse and the system starts all over again.

I received this question from a reader on my blog.

> *What should I do if my spouse refuses to acknowledge his emotional online affair? He says I'm overreacting. He stopped contacting her, but not out of remorse or of wanting to do the right thing. He just wants me off his back. He refuses to go to counseling with me so I go by myself. Also, he won't talk to anyone about this issue. I am afraid that without talking about our relationship, the same thing will happen again. He still plays regularly on the game site he met her on, even though I have told him it makes me nervous. I caught him talking to her last month. I feel like a doormat. He is in a state of withdrawal and denial about what he has done. I have read that this is called an emotional divorce. I am trying to find out how I can meet his needs that I was not meeting before, even though he won't tell me what they are, and I'm studying God's word to give me strength. I believe God has brought me into a marriage covenant that He does not desire to be broken. My husband has built a wall around his heart that is very hard, and I believe he has allowed Satan to lie to him. I feel I need to win him back, but this is so backwards. I was the one betrayed, but he is the one who is full of anger and bitterness because I "took away his good friend."*

Let's take a look at what is going on. I speak to my female colleagues at work. We laugh and talk about our weekends, but I do not sit across from them and play chess privately while no one else is around. This would be very inappropriate and it is, in effect, what he is doing. In his mind, he has justified the behavior as harmless, but apparently, an emotional bond has been established, and this is infidelity in its most deceptive form. His actions are very harmful, as an intimate connection has been made with someone other than his wife. He may believe he's having harmless fun. If his conversations are not intimate, then he is. He's having harmless fun with a woman that is not you. This is a problem. There is a perception that when there's no physical contact, there's no affair. This is false. It's at least an emotional affair. Well, how do you reach a spouse who does not acknowledge the extramarital relationship for what it is?

The issue must be discussed, but you pose a difficult predicament since he will not talk to anyone about it. Someone or something has to make him see what he's done. Hopefully he'll become remorseful, but even if he doesn't, if he decides to stay off the game, and talk about what is going on, the rebuilding of your marriage can begin. Otherwise, you will simply become roommates.

Here are some things that I think you should do. First, there is an emotional need that he is getting met from the game and from her. You mentioned that you haven't met his needs in the past, so he may be expecting you to act the way you did then. This may be difficult, but keep meeting his needs even while he is neglecting yours. If you start meeting his needs now, he will hopefully begin noticing the difference. "In the same way, you wives, be submissive to your own husbands so that even if any of them are disobedient to the word, they may be won without a word by the behavior of their wives, as they observe your chaste and respectful behavior." (1 Peter 3:1, 2) Actions speak louder than words. Second, keep praying (especially when he's on the computer) and trust in God's timing. Ask your friends and relatives to pray at those particular times too.

What you don't want to do is go at him aggressively and verbally attack him. This is what you want to do and maybe what he deserves, but he will become defensive and not listen, which is the opposite of what you want. So, third, I would recommend sitting down with him and telling him exactly how you feel. He needs to know what this has done to you emotionally, and what you think it has done to your marriage. Make sure you do it from the standpoint of, "This is how I feel and what I think has happened" rather than "This is how you (husband) messed up!!" Use "I" statements like, "It hurts me when we don't spend time together." Don't say, "Why are you always on that computer with her?" "Why" questions make people defensive. If you were my clients, I would ask him, "For your life to be just like you want it, what would have to change?" Maybe you can do this. Maybe he'll open up. Also, don't do it every night. His wall must be torn down with the power of God not with repeated onslaughts.

Well, how long do you go until you say, "I'm through!" This is between you and God. Infidelity is cause for divorce (Matthew 5:32). However, with your son, and with what you've already built, divorcing will have its own set of difficulties. You may trade one problem for another, but with the prospect of winning him back, you must decide how much you are willing to work. You're trying to save your marriage, but there are souls involved here, also. Like I said, this is between you and God. Threatening with divorce may be what shakes him conscious, but I can't be sure of that.

Satan does win some over, but hopefully with prayer, your husband's heart can be changed.

AFFAIRS AFFECT EVERYONE

Extramarital affairs are devastating to everyone. The betrayed spouse, kids, immediate family, and even friends and coworkers bear the brunt of this earth-shattering event.

After the infidelity is discovered, the unfaithful often say, "We never intended for this to happen." True. Most spouses, when leaving for work, don't set out to come home having begun an inappropriate relationship. However, things like this don't just happen; many factors contribute.

There's a commercial on television for the Plan B pill. It is a contraception that stops a pregnancy before it begins. Their slogan is, "Because the unexpected happens." I'm sure the unexpected does, but I can't help but think when I see this TV spot, "If you have unprotected sex, you could get pregnant. What did you think would happen? Were you sleeping in health class?" The same is true with affairs. While someone may never set out to have an affair, if you neglect your spouse and develop an attraction to someone else, what do you think is going to happen?

Another response is, "It just happened." This statement, as well as the first, minimizes the events leading to the affair and also the hurtful ripple affect that will be felt for years. It's like saying that September 11, "just happened." Both statements give little credence to what has occurred and both are quite maddening to the betrayed.

Many marriages end when an affair takes place, but if you decide to work things out, there are some things that must occur. The offending spouse must grasp the extent of his or her behavior, and this understanding must be communicated to the hurting spouse. An emphatic understanding is key.

In regards to the offended spouse, his/her part in this must be seen as well. Maybe he or she spent too much time doing something else. Oftentimes an affair can be the result of what both spouses have or have not done.

If you decide to work things out, keep in mind that it is a great deal of work. I have a slogan on my office wall that says, "Every true strength is gained through struggle." Things can get better.

We're human and we must work on what is before us, so avoid the affair, and have an affair with your spouse. Meet him at a hotel or do something surprising like prepare dinner for her. The newness will set a fire aflame, and the simple idea that you thought ahead will do wonders for your relationship.

DENIAL

Let's say that you just found out you're spouse is having an affair. You are deeply pained. What is his/her reaction and where does it take you and your relationship?

When you address the issue with your spouse, he/she can have one of two reactions. First, he could admit to his error, and you can both begin the process

of healing. It's not easy to do, but you are thankful that he sees his place in the matter and is willing to take responsibility. The other path he could take is this: turning the tables. Where once you were angry because he did something wrong; you suddenly feel guilty. You're not sure why this is, but before you know it, you find yourself apologizing. You are working to sooth his now upset emotional state. Later, you think, "What just happened?"

Like a crying child caught with chocolate brownie all over her face, your spouse has turned the tide of blame away from her (where it belongs) and on to you. By making you angry and confused, she transfers the blame. Her threats of leaving or other behaviors frighten you and you relent. You are now the one apologizing and asking her to be happy again. What have you done? You have accepted the responsibility for something that is clearly not your fault.

Well, maybe you are doing something. No one is perfect. Think about it and listen to what she tells you. Later, when you are calm, consider what she says and work to make necessary changes. We all could be better spouses. However, this does not mean you should take the blame for something that is clearly her fault. While your lack of attention towards her made her lonely, she actually chose the affair over other options. You did not. She chose to do what she did and no amount of blaming can change this. Promise to do better. Promise to be a more attentive spouse, but do not carry the burden that says you are the cause of the infraction.

What's going on with your spouse? Well, she is selfish and childish. She can't handle the negative feelings that go along with guilt so she "flips the script" and suddenly she's the victim because you brought the subject up. You are hurting her. Why would you do this? This shows immaturity, and a lack of character on her part. This behavior can be very detrimental to the marriage.

What else is happening? Your spouse is angry with himself and suddenly you are the object of his anger. While anger can be a natural expression of guilt, it isn't necessarily a healthy one as an angry mind is often a clouded mind. By choosing anger, he isn't choosing the best method to solve the problem and fix what should be fixed. Instead, he blows up, blames you and hopes you'll just forget about it. The experience he has caused was so uncomfortable; don't dismiss it. Don't forget about it. Misbehavior on the part of your husband or wife at this level could be a sign that you need counseling. If he continues to transfer the burden of guilt on to you, you'll eventually get tired and calloused towards his behavior. Rather than growing closer, you are growing apart.

There is one area where you are at fault. You allowed this to happen. When you know you are right (and you better be abundantly sure on this) stand your ground and force him or her to accept their responsibility. Otherwise, you'll continue to be a parent wiping the chocolate brownie off the face of a guilty child, whether it's an affair or something else.

Chapter 13 – Love is an Action

"Love doesn't commit suicide. We have to kill it. Though, it's true that it often simply dies of our neglect." -*Diane Sollee*

—

At this point hopefully, you've made some decisions about where you are in your marriage. You have an idea of what steps you need to take in order to improve your relationship. I have outlined the nuts and bolts of things, but something I can't do for you now is put in the effort. It's up to you to work to the level you want to be in.

The world says that love is what I want for me. The world says that love is a feeling, but 1 Corinthians 13 tells us what love is, and it's a collection of behaviors. Are you doing the opposite of what Paul tells us in this very important chapter? Consider this:

Love is impatient, love is mean and it is selfish. Love brags to others and thinks a lot of itself. Love acts out around others to embarrass them. Love gets angry easily and remembers every wrong that has ever happened. Love gets excited when sin is around and works to make up lies. Love quits when things get hard.

If your wife has ever said you are impatient, that means you are not communicating love to her. If your husband has ever told you that you embarrass him, he is telling you that you aren't acting in a very loving way.

Love is a decision, but the feelings associated with love can't be denied. They are important, and we want to have them. These feelings were easy to come by early in the relationship, but something has happened and those feelings are long gone. If you commit to acting from a loving standpoint, the feelings will eventually return. Commit to changing your behaviors and your relationship will change.

Have you ever heard or uttered the phrase, "I love you, I'm just not in love with you?" What does this mean? You either love someone or you don't. This statement seems to indicate a gap between how someone feels and how someone thinks they should feel. Obstacles have entered the relationship and created a gulf. How can one span this chasm?

First, you must recognize that you can create a feeling of love for someone that you think you have lost it for. Love is a decision wherein actions turn into feelings.

Second, what created the gulf? Maybe it was created by a si

mistake. Maybe it was created by a lot of little mistakes such as

neglect. Maybe the leap seems too large because your spouse is

just too bitter/angry/unfaithful.

Finally, decide that if you want to be "in love" with that

person, commit to changing your behavior and hopefully he or

she will follow your lead to a better relationship.

In my practice I can instruct and help people change their

behaviors, but unless they put forth the effort, their behaviors

won't change and neither will their hearts. The heart can be tricky

because it may have scars that no one sees or realizes. Also, the

person who needs to change may be tired of trying and lack the

motivation. He or she has been hurt enough and her heart is just

done. There may be nothing that can reach the them. When this

happens, the person must make an intellectual decision to shape

their behaviors, which can result in a more loving relationship.

WORK ON YOUR MARRIAGE

Consider 1 Peter 3 and its instructions in suffering for doing

good. I don't believe that marriage is suffering, but it can

occasionally be a part of it since we sacrifice and humble

ourselves to the point of meeting another needs. Because

marriage will not always be easy, we must consider suffering as

spoken of in Romans 3:3-5, " . . . we also exult in our tribulations,

knowing that tribulation brings about perseverance; and

perseverance, proven character; and proven character, hope; and hope does not disappoint . . . ." Going through difficult times can bring us closer together. This is the part in our vows when we said, "or worse." Growing and learning together can be difficult. So, understanding that it can help your marriage is an important lesson

Peter tells us to be harmonious. Spouses seem intent sometimes on being at war. I have spoken to several couples who are choosing to fight. The conflict is simple and not terribly important, but because both want to be right. They argue over how the dishes are placed in the dishwasher, who drives the better car and who makes more money. Two people who should be working together are doing anything but being harmonious. Choose this over arguing.

We should also be sympathetic towards one another. When one spouse is down, you don't hurt them or relish in their difficulties. When they win, you win. If they lose, you lose. Don't find pleasure in their bad days or misfortune.

Next, we learn to be brotherly. How can a husband and wife be brotherly? Well, with men that I have had brotherly relationships with, we could be brutally honest with one another. If one believes the other is living wrong, we can speak to them about it. The person could do nothing, or say nothing that would make me stop appreciating him and being his brother. I've never been in the military, but I understand these guys could be fist fighting one moment, and be willing to die for one another the next. Brotherly love means we go through difficult times together; we don't drop the person and walk away when things get tough.

Are you kindhearted? Some spouses need to be reminded of this. You are supposed to be kind to one another. I had one particular couple that struggled with this, and they ended up getting tattoos that said, "Kinder Words." Ironically (or purposefully), it was on the inside of their right wrists, the very spot that would be exposed were they to point at the other and begin a barrage of hurtful words.

To be kind hearted, you must be humble in spirit because you are thinking of the other person. You aren't putting yourself and your needs first. Matthew 5:3 says, "Blessed are the poor in spirit, for theirs is the kingdom of heaven." Humility is a key factor in the Christian life and in your marriage.

Peter continues in verse nine and says we shouldn't return evil for evil or insult for insult, yet this characterizes many marriages. Instead, we should work to be a blessing to one another as the verse continues. This can be difficult in marriage when you both seem to be at war. One of you must extend the olive branch of peace. One of you must be the first to move for change. Then, hopefully your spouse will follow your lead. Verse 9 ends by saying that if we do this, we will inherit a blessing and isn't this what our marriages should be? A blessing.

COME TOGETHER

Sometimes couples get into such a state that they are extremely divided, but because of one spouse's level of commitment, he or she refuses to quit on the relationship. Certainly, there may be a time to quit. But at this time, one of the spouses has resolved to save the marriage. It can be done. As I've said before, you're never too far-gone in your marriage if you're willing to make the journey back. So, what should a spouse do if he/she wants to save the marriage?

First, is it worth saving? If your partner is on his/her 20th affair, should you keep going? Only you can answer that. Anybody can change at any time and Jesus teaches us in Matthew 18 to have no limit on our forgiveness, but there should be a limit to the degree we are going to endure poor marital behavior. How much is that for you? Decide, and then move forward.

Second, if it is worth saving, what are you saving it for? There must be a motivator and in a chaotic state, any will do. Children come to mind first. They are better off in a home where mom and dad learn to love one another than in a home void of this love. So, if you are doing it for your children, make sure you do it right. You might also consider the material investments you've made in the marriage. Remember, any motivator will do and starting over on what you've done so far to earn it is pretty scary.

Third, you must work to change the narrative in the home. For weeks or months your relationship has been built on the negative. "We wouldn't be in this mess if you hadn't . . ." is what you might say. What is wrong in the marriage must be discussed, but do it during controlled times that you agree upon. Also, if you learn how to communicate about difficult topics, the discussions can be just that, discussions rather than arguments which only make the problem worse. Localize the negative, deal with it, and make the rest of your home life positive and encouraging.

Finally, you must now change the behavior in the marriage. If you are not the offending spouse, this means acting out of love (not obligation) for your lover. If you are the offending spouse, this means going overboard on showing your spouse that you have nothing to hide. In either case, changing behavior to look like a happy marriage results in being a happy marriage. It became unhappy because you were doing all the wrong things. Now, you must act differently. This "fake it til you make it" method can work and eventually be sincere.

Marriages are worth saving. If yours is one of these, begin the journey to *Your Best Marriage*, today.

Made in United States
Orlando, FL
28 December 2023